I0616617

Give God Your Broken Pieces: 30 Day Devotional

Jelia Coleman-Hepner

Acknowledgments

I wrote this devotional to help with spiritual growth and up-lift individuals going through life storms. I must acknowledge some of my friends and family who helped me get to this point in my life.

I want to thank my aunt dot, Dorothy Fillmore, for speaking life over me in 2012 when I went back to school. She told me that I had great talent and would be a writer one day. Her words and love always kept me going, even when I questioned my purpose.

A big thank you to my writing mentor Professor Alanna Miller at Fayetteville State University, who guided me during my time in college.

Also, I have to acknowledge my great friend Nikki Davis who has been a great support system. Her faith and allowing God to use her have changed my life, and I am forever grateful. When I told her I felt God was telling me to write this devotional, she had nothing but encouraging words and told me, "Your writing God will use to bless others." Thank you for your faith in me and giving me a platform when I first started. May you continue to put greatness on this earth.

Thank you so much for loving me to my children, Jayvon, Jaylen, and Jahnay. All my kids supported me, but my daughter Jahnay went the extra mile to listen to my ideas, read over my writings, and give me her opinions. I love you guys, and you are why I continue to strive for greatness.

And I can't leave out my friends and family for always being on my side and supporting me in whatever I do. Thank you so much for always supporting my ideas and creations to my mom, family, and friends.

Remember God will place the right people in your life to fulfill your purpose.

Dear God,

Thank you for giving me the love and the patience for writing. I pray this will help your children on this earth,

Amen.

Be Who You Are

POST to Be

I previously worked with a woman who constantly posted scriptures and Godly quotes/memes on her social media almost daily. When viewing her posts, not knowing her personally at the time, I would think to myself, *man, she is just a positive person who really loves God and uplifting others.*

After a few weeks of training at this job, I had the opportunity to work side by side with her. Finally, I was able to get a better insight into who she was personally. Needless to say, it was like working with Dr. Jekyll and Mr. Hyde. Every word out of her mouth was a curse word, she spoke negatively about other co-workers, had a bad attitude, displayed confrontational behavior, and so much more.

Now let me say this, no one walking this earth is perfect. We all have flaws and areas in our lives we need to work on. Yet there is a big variation in posting a Bible verse in the morning, and by lunch, you have cussed out two people or have a reputation of fighting when your anger gets to a certain level.

1

It's important we, as followers of Christ, be who we POST to be. Not only because it pleases God, but you never know who is observing you. Some people may want to become believers or are at the beginning stages of their walk with Christ. They can see you posting Christ-like things on social media but acting differently in person. This could either turn people off from wanting to follow Christ, bring doubt on the faith, or make a person believe it's okay to act like you are one way and be another way.

"Be imitators of me, as I am of Christ."- 1 Corinthians 11:1

When it comes to this life journey, the walk will never be perfect, but we have choices regarding how we carry ourselves in the social media world.

"In the same way, let your light shine before others so that they may see your good works and give glory to your Father, who is in heaven." - Matthew 5:16

God never gives extra brownie points because you post Bible quotes or positive messages. He only cares about your heart! He cares if you are really living the word or just trying to impress your followers.

So, remember to be who you are POST to be.

Give God Your Broken

Pieces

One day, I remember going to the Social Services office to
apply for medical and food assistance. I was sitting in
a room with five other people, waiting to be called by
my chosen caseworker. Eight months pregnant, I was sitting in the back,
glancing out of a window filled with a broken spirit. I kept asking myself,
"How did you get here?" My husband (at the time) walked out on me for
another woman, leaving me pregnant, with no vehicle, no money, and a set
of twins who were already five years old to take care of by myself. Being
forced to go back to my hometown to stay with my mother added embarrassment to the pain. I sat there with so many emotions rushing through
me, wanting to die, feeling empty, hurt, humiliated, lonely, and the list goes
on.

While sitting there, the woman who signed me in sat in a corner at
the room's front. She called my name, and I looked up at her, assuming she
would tell me something pertaining to my appointment. She removed her
glasses off her face, looked directly at me, and said, "Jelia, God told me to

tell you He hears you, and everything will be okay." I could not help it; at that moment, I broke into tears.

The night before, I kept praying, crying, and screaming out to God, asking Him, *"Why me?"* I begged Him for a sign. I said, *"Please reveal to me You are with me and hear me. "*Understand this, I had never seen this lady in my life, and nobody knew about my situation. All I did was walk in, smile, sign my name on a clipboard, and sit down. Nobody could ever convince me that wasn't God.

This moment changed my life, showed me God's love for me is real. My soul and my heart were empty, but He met me in the depths of my brokenness. While my situation did not change overnight, God sent a "life ring" to me while drowning in the sea of life. If He did it for me, then I know He will do it for you.

"He heals the brokenhearted and binds up their wounds." – Psalm 147:3

Even if the situation is breaking you, or is because of something you created, it doesn't matter. God is full of mercy and grace. All He requires of you is to come to Him, lay your burdens (depression, anxiety, pain, and brokenness), at His feet, and He will take it from there.

"The righteous cry out, and the Lord hears and delivers them out of all their troubles." – Psalm 34:17

We must learn to give our broken pieces to God. Whether its divorce, depression, loss of a loved one, facing an illness, or having a child on drugs, just give it to God almighty.

I understand you are weary, damaged, and want to give up, but know God sees and hears you. He is working in your favor, even when you cannot see it. While waiting on God to heal you or change your circumstances, this is the opportunity to immerse yourself into Bible reading, prayer, faith, fasting, and finding various ways to worship Him.

The devil desires you to have doubt, he loves it when you are hurt or feel defeated. He takes those moments to attack and crush you. Remember, you are in Christ, and nothing can harm you because you are God's child.

"The Lord will rescue me from every evil attack and will bring me safely to His heavenly kingdom. To Him, the glory forever and ever. Amen." – 2 Timothy 4:18.

He hears your cries, recognizes your frustration, and feels your pain. No matter how broken you are, replace your feelings with faith, and allow the Potter to put you back together again.

Did You Ask God First?

I recall a situation when my associate came to me about a business idea she had. She was tired of working at her current job and felt it was time to start working for herself. Being the supportive person I am, I told her to go for it. She can do anything she sets her mind to. Later that evening, the Holy Spirit convicted me of what I had done. He said, "Who gave you the authority to stamp her plan? Why did you not tell her to pray about it and seek Me first?"

Now when this happened, I can't lie; I was in my feelings. I conversed with God telling Him my side and how I was only trying to be a good supporter. Yet, after thinking about it, my heart was in the right place, but the way I went about it was not the best.

As humans, it's in our nature to encourage ourselves and others to chase dreams, desires, and goals. Everywhere we turn, our culture says to be a boss, chase the bag, or reach your dreams at all costs. The only problem is before we begin doing all of that, when do we stop, go to God, and make sure the route we are about to take is in His will for us? Sometimes we are so focused on OUR passions and what we DESIRE that we never stop to make sure it's what God wants.

"For I know the plans I have for you," declares the LORD.

"Plans to prosper you and not to harm you, plans to give you hope and a future." – Jeremiah 29:11

God knows your desires and what path is good for you and what's not. We have to fully trust Him and seek His confirmation first before we make any life choices. Many of us may have decided to do something in the past, and it was not of God's will. That's why things fall apart, fail, or the choice we make ends up bringing more stress to our lives than before.

Many of us do things backward; we go ahead and pursue what we want and then ask God to bless it after we already did it. That's not building a healthy relationship with our heavenly father and can cause you various heartaches or confusion in life. Also, if you are not careful, the choice you make can end up being a distraction and pulling you farther away from the will of God.

It's okay to tell yourself, friends, or family, to chase dreams or desired goals. Make sure during the conversation you add for them to seek God first and see what He says about it. Whether it is buying a car, house, getting married/ dating, moving to another city, or starting a business, it doesn't matter how big or small; seek confirmation and clarity.

"Trust in the Lord with all your heart; do not depend on your understanding. Seek His will in all you do, and He will show you which path to take." – Proverbs 3:5-6

Don't Go Down Without a Fight!

I remember growing up and hearing parents tell their child if they go to school and get beat up by a bully, when they come home, they will get another beating. While I disagree with this method, I do understand where the thought comes from. Nobody wants their child to get beat up, run, or hide from a bully.

In a way, God is like this toward us! God is our parent, and the devil is the bully; our God doesn't want us to keep coming to him crying without fighting back.

I am not talking about fighting physically in the flesh; I mean fighting back spiritually.

For we do not wrestle against flesh and blood, but against the rulers, against the authorities, against the cosmic powers over this present darkness, against the spiritual forces of evil in the heavenly places. – Ephesians 6:12

When your boss is mistreating you, your spouse or children are acting up, someone in your family or maybe someone you work with is spreading lies about you; all those are spiritual attacks—the devil attacks in ways such as physically and mentally. Your marriage, job, relationships, family, or feelings can be nothing but a playing field for the devil to use to execute his plans.

Learn to fight back! Instead of allowing the devil to win by just crying, getting upset, or complaining, do something about it.

Do more than just pray, read scriptures aloud, speak aloud and tell the devil he can't win! Post scriptures around your house or prayer closet and fast. If you need to use holy water, do so.

I heard a story about a young man working in a hostile environment. He would go home to his wife and complain about how bad his boss was mistreating everyone. One day, he felt God told him he needed to fight back and do more. So, he decided to fast; he prayed at a specific time every morning; he even got up early to beat everyone to the office to start placing holy water over his boss's door. After months of prayer, actions and continuing to be a good worker, he said God came through with a breakthrough, and something happened causing her to be nice to all the employees, even buying doughnuts once a week.

Your storms or circumstances may be different, but the point is to fight back. Put the armor of God on every day you wake up.

"Put on the whole armor of God. That ye may be able to stand against the wiles of the devil." - Ephesians 6:11

Get up and say, devil, you can't have my _____ (fill in the blank).

For example, devil, you can't have my husband!

Devil, you can't have my child!

Devil, you can't have my boss!

Devil, you can't have my mind!

Whatever it is, say it aloud, read scriptures aloud, pray aloud. Wake those demons up and let them know they can't bully their way into your life, and you are prepared to fight back with Jesus by your side. And if you feel like you are too weak or just too frustrated, then it's okay because God will step in to fight for you!

Learn to fight back and put your foot on the devil's neck to let him know you're not going down without a fight, no matter what the situation is.

Enjoying the Single Phase

I could not tell you how often I have complained to my friends and family about being single. Observing numerous couples on social media or being around friends in relationships can add to your loneliness. At one point, I was even tired of hearing, "Be patient; God will send you someone," from individuals around me trying to give encouraging words.

One day while watching a YouTube sermon, I heard this pastor say, "Enjoy your single phase because God is doing something this season." This stuck with me. I never thought of it that way. I never realized the changes I was going through in my season of singleness. I prayed more, spent more time with God, learned how to heal from past trauma, and spent more time with family and friends. Yet I could not see any of this because I was so busy focusing on my desire to have someone in my life. I overlooked the impact God was making in my life during this season because I was too busy complaining instead of praising Him.

"Delight yourself in the Lord, and He will give you the desires of your heart." Psalm 37:4

I know your heart desires for you to be in a relationship but understand this is the time to draw near to Jesus. He wants to do some work inside you while you are single. When God makes you wait, it's always for a reason; He builds you up by working on issues you carry around (known or unknown). Factors such as your temper, lack of faith, decision-making, prayer life, insecurities, childhood trauma, or other negative issues can explain why God is having you wait.

Sometimes we are walking "red flags" ourselves and don't even recognize it, and other times He is trying to protect us from others who are "red flags." So, take this season you are by yourself and seek His face. He will reveal the areas He wants you to change or improve on before you meet your mate.

Focus on praying, fasting, seeking a relationship with God, and living in your purpose because when you do, you won't have time to focus on your singleness. He knows and loves you, so He will place the right person in your path when the time is right, in the right season.

"To everything, there is a season, and a time to every purpose under the heaven." - Ecclesiastes 3:1

Facing Childhood Trauma

When I was a child, I knew a girl who was subjected to molestation for many years. It was something she hid from family and friends because of who it was and how it made her feel. Today she is thirty-six and is now realizing its effects on her throughout this journey called life.

She became a people pleaser, formed PTSD (Post-Traumatic Stress Disorder), had low self-esteem, and would allow men to come into her life and use her emotionally and physically because she would rather suffer in silence than be alone. While growing up, she also hurt people due to the pain of just wanting to be loved, no matter how deep the measures would be to get it.

We must face childhood trauma, or some people would call it "demons." As the great Dr. Phil once said, "You can't fix or heal if you never face the trauma."

I don't know what happened in your childhood; you could have been teased a lot, parents got divorced, physically or sexually abused, abandoned, didn't get the love and recognition from a parent you thought you deserved, whatever the case is, you have to face it.

I had a friend tell me he is promiscuous because, as a child, he would watch his father beat his mother and then beat him almost nightly. He had anger toward women because he thought his mother should have left the situation and focus on protecting him and his siblings. So, he slept with many women because he felt he controlled the situation, numbed the pain, and no woman was worth respect because of what he witnessed growing up.

Many of us are like him; we are aware of trauma from our childhood we never faced, and its effects on decisions we make in our adulthood, but we don't take steps to heal. We keep it moving or say, "This is how I am."

If you want to please God and live your life for the kingdom, you must give your pain and past to Him. First, forgive yourself for the things you did or allowed because of your pain but then forgive the person(s) who caused your trauma.

"Come to me, all you who are weary and burdened, and I will give you rest." - Matthew 11:28

Give Jesus your anger, sadness, anxiety, pain, resentment, whatever negative feelings you have; give it all to him. Let our savior heal your heart and change the negative things you do in life due to your childhood trauma. Also, if you don't think you recognize anything, ask God to show you any negative parts of your childhood affecting you.

"He heals the brokenhearted and binds up their wounds." - Psalm 147:3

I don't know why God sometimes chooses certain people to go through specific battles, but I know He is a healer, and you are never alone. Trust Jesus. Go to Him and ask Him to fix it and know God will also give you signs if you need extra assistance such as therapy. Believe, have faith, and trust the process but make sure you face it.

Finding Hope While Suffering in Silence

I read this article about a beautiful young lady who won the Miss USA pageant in 2019. After posting the message, "I hope this day brings you peace," on Instagram, she decided to go to the ninth floor of a high-rise building in New York City and jump to her death. Looking on the outside, it seemed like she had it all together. She was beautiful, had fame, had a lot of social media followers, and traveled the world. It seemed (especially on social media) she had the life many dreamed of.

In an interview, her mother said her daughter suffered from depression and dreaded turning thirty. Her suicide brought heavy awareness to individuals who have the appearance of having everything together on the surface but are suffering emotionally in silence.

Thousands of people go to bed every night praying they don't wake up because they have lost hope. Everyday struggles such as sickness, childhood trauma, divorce, family issues, financial struggles, and other real-life challenges can test anyone's faith. While many of us judge others by their smiles, we assume people have good lives if it looks good on social media.

But there are people who walk around feeling emotionally dead. Once people get to that point in life, they can lose hope.

The dictionary states the word "hope" is the expectation and desire for a sure thing to happen or a feeling of trust. Hope is a part of trusting God, knowing whatever situation you are facing; He will turn it around.

"For I know the plans I have for you," declares the Lord. "Plans to prosper you and not harm you, plans to give you hope and a future. – Jeremiah 29:11

I know it can be easy for others who are not facing your storm to tell you to continue to have faith and hope when you want to give up. Every day, it takes your strength to even get out of bed. You must know you are strong, and God has built you for this. I know you are tired; you feel weak and like it's unfair, but nothing will compare to the blessing coming in your life if you don't give up.

"He gives strength to the weary and increases the power of the weak. Even youths grow tired and weary, and young men stumble and fall, but those who hope in the Lord will renew their strength. They will soar on wings like eagles; they will run and not grow weary; they will walk and not be faint." – Isaiah 40:29-31

God needs you to fully trust Him because when you don't, it opens up a door to doubt, depression, suicidal thoughts, loneliness, sadness, and even a loss of faith. Every life battle is different, and if you feel stuck in a dark place for a long time, it's okay to reach out for help. God created therapists for a reason, as a tool to help us get through the hard times. It's not always easy to get through storms, especially when it has been going on for months or even years but know God has a plan and He is in the midst of your battle. Continue to pray, fast, trust, and seek Him especially when you don't feel like it. When you feel like giving up or like this "Christian religion" is not working, continue to have hope because He will NEVER let you down, even when you are suffering in silence.

Fix Your Focus Before You Sink

Most of us know the Bible story of the miracle Jesus performed with his disciple Peter, after the feeding of the five thousand. During a bad storm at sea, Jesus appeared to the disciples while walking on water. Peter wanted to prove himself to Jesus, so he said, *"Lord if it is You, command me to come to You on the water," Matthew 14:28.* Stepping out of the boat into the sea's rough waters, Peter kept his eye on Jesus but suddenly started to sink. Why did Peter sink? It's because he took his eyes off Jesus, which allowed fear and doubt to creep in.

We are just like Peter sometimes. We go through life storms such as financial difficulties, losing a job, health issues, death, relationship problems, or loneliness, and we take our eyes off God. Our vision shifts to our circumstances. When this happens, we open the door to the enemy. This allows him to invade our thoughts with fear, sadness, anxiety, and doubt, along with other negativity.

This can be one of your most challenging seasons or toughest battles, with trouble on every corner, but you must always keep your focus on Jesus. When Peter cried out, Jesus quickly reached out his hand and took hold of him, saying, *"You of little faith, why are you so afraid?"* *Matthew 8:26.* Then Jesus rebuked the winds and the waves, and it was completely calm.

If He can do it for Peter, He most definitely, without question, will do it for you. At any moment, Jesus is going to rebuke your storm and calm the rough waves in your life. He hears your cries; he knows your worries; He knows every problem you face every day you wake up. You must keep the faith and believe He will take care of any situation.

"Cast all your anxiety on Him because He cares for you." - 1 Peter 5:7

Whatever you are going through, know God will always keep His word. In due time and season, He will come through! Just continue to praise Him every day, spend time in His presence, have faith the size of a mustard seed, and keep your focus on Jesus, so you will not end up sinking.

Dear God,

Catch My Thoughts!

A friend of mine told me sometimes, when she wakes up in the mornings, she feels overwhelmed with depressing thoughts. She described it as a heavy blanket of negativity just laying on her the moment she opens her eyes. I informed her it was one of the tactics of the enemy. See, the enemy anticipates you opening your eyes every morning because he knows he can destroy your whole day or night with the right ammunition. The devil has no boundaries, whether it's early in the morning, evening, or night, he aims for your mind.

Nine out of ten times, once you catch a negative thought, one thought becomes a link connected to another connection, which will become a chain of destructive thoughts.

For example, if you recently had a job interview and ended up not getting the job, you might start a chain of negative thoughts like this:

"Why didn't I get the job?"

Then, *"What's wrong with me?"* followed by, *"I could have said this instead of that."*

21

It will continue with, *"If that company did not want me, maybe I am not good enough."*

Do you see the negative chain? One negative thought just became several negative thoughts within a matter of seconds.

The devil knows if he can get to you mentally with negativity, it opens the door to sadness, depression, apathy, anxiety, fear, and more.

One of my favorite Pastors, Steven Furtick, said in a sermon, "Before I caught a feeling, I caught a thought."

This is a remarkable statement because our feelings or mood always starts with a thought.

What if we started giving our thoughts to God? As soon as you have the first negative thought, how about you say, "God, negative thinking just approach my mind. Instead of pondering on it more, I give this thought to you in exchange for a positive one."

Thou wilt keep him in perfect peace, whose mind is stayed on Thee; because he trusteth in Thee. – Isaiah 26:3

This is not to say other factors in your life, such as unemployment, sickness, breakup, death, or financial woes, won't play into these feelings. I'm saying there are ways to limit these feelings by controlling negative thoughts we encounter.

This isn't going to change your circumstance overnight, but this is a way to help you get through it. Festering on negative thoughts never helped anyone's situation. It won't make you feel better; it won't take the pain away, so why not start giving it to Jesus?

Cast all your anxiety on Him because He cares for you. - 1 Peter 5:7

And He does care for you; He wants to destroy those negative thoughts. He wants us to run to Him and let Him protect our mind from the enemy. That's why we must practice a good prayer life. So, when these moments approach, we will run toward Him in prayer and learn to change our thinking habits.

So today, let's start. As soon as a negative thought comes into your mind, go to Him, and say, "God catch this!"

God, I Praise You Even If.......

"**G**od, I praise you even if," is a powerful statement! On this journey of life, we value the things God does for us. We pray for something every day, whether it's for protection for our family, better career opportunities, saving a broken marriage/relationship, to get an increase in finances and the list goes on, but will you praise Him if you don't get what you pray for?

You can pray for various situations, and it does not turn out the way you desire. You ask for the healing of a loved one, and they still die from sickness. You pray God restores a marriage, but the divorce still happens. Asking for a better job, you end up getting laid off. You and your spouse have been praying to have a child, but instead, you keep experiencing miscarriages.

Can you still praise Him during the storms, even when challenging life situations come?

In Psalm 34, David reminds us we should praise God through the good times and bad. Praise should fill our hearts every day, no matter our circumstances, especially when walking through seasons of great trials.

"I will praise the Lord, who counsels me; even at night, my heart instructs me. I keep my eyes always on the Lord. With Him at my right hand, I will not be shaken."- Psalm 16:7-8

Praising Jesus when everything is going right is easy, yet we need to praise Him even when things are wrong. Praising Him during the storms tells Jesus even though you are going through the fire, you fully trust Him. You trust even if He closes a door or doesn't answer a prayer in the way you wanted, He has bigger plans than you ever imagined.

No matter how upset you get because your prayers were not answered in the way you envisioned, God has greater plans.

"For I know the plans I have for you," declares the LORD, "plans to prosper you and not to harm you, plans to give you hope and a future." - Jeremiah 29:11

You have to believe and have complete faith in God everything will work out to His glory. If you did not get the job, He has a better one. If you have been single for years, God will send you a spouse in due time. You may have lost a loved one, but He might have a plan for you to lead and help others who lost someone. You might not have gotten a raise at work because He wants to teach you stewardship over what you already have. We never know God's plan until it happens, but we have to keep the faith and praise Him regardless. If you are the type who gets upset and stops talking to Jesus when trials come, don't worry He still loves you. Just ask for forgiveness and ask Him to strengthen your heart and faith so you are anchored, even if things don't go your way.

You have to get so strong with your faith you get up every morning and say, "God, I praise you even if..."

God is the Problem Solver

My daughter decided to change things up and dye her hair this ginger color one year. After coming from the salon, she told me she hated the color, and all she did was wear a hoodie and cry about it. After letting her sulk for a few days, I sat her down so we could talk. I told her I understood she was in the stage of her life where she was about to be in college, and she could make decisions independently. Yet, I asked her if she felt she messed up or things did not come out as expected, then why not come to me for advice or allow me to help her with the issue.

How many of us are like this with Christ? We make decisions and the results don't come out as planned, but instead of going to God about it, we cry or hide from Him. Jesus loves you, and no wrong decision or sin can separate you from His love.

"For I am sure that neither death nor life, nor angels nor rulers, nor things present nor things to come, nor powers, nor height nor depth, nor anything else in all creation, will be able to separate us from the love of God in Christ Jesus our Lord." - Romans 8:38-39

God doesn't want you to feel embarrassed, ashamed, or sad about your choices and not come to Him about it. Regardless of whose bed you were in last night, what drugs you did, who you gossiped or lied to, the porn you watched, or whatever the case is, Jesus wants you to repent and come to Him so he can fix it. It can even be minor things like making a wrong financial decision causing more debt or accepting an offer for a job position without seeking God's approval first. A big or small decision turning out bad is okay because Christ is a father, and His job is to care for us any way He can, but we have to come to Him first and give Him the situation, instead of trying to fix it ourselves or sit and cry or pout about it.

"Casting all your anxieties on Him, because He cares for you." - 1 Peter 5:7

That's your Father, and He wants to have a relationship with you where you can come to Him about ANYTHING. And I mean ANYTHING! Don't be like my daughter and pout or cry about your situation. Seek out the problem solver and let Him solve all your problems.

Have Strong Community

Some years ago, I went hiking up a mountain with friends, and during the journey, one of my friends had to make several stops to rest during the hike. She stated she was out of shape, and the hike was taking a lot out of her mentally and physically. Once we reached the top of the mountain, she thanked everyone in the group for pushing her. She said everyone giving her encouraging words, walking with her, and telling her she could do it, is what kept her pushing.

This situation made me realize how important having a good community, or a strong circle of friends is. Everyone will face seasons and trials. We will need people in our corner to encourage or push us. No person was built to go through this journey alone, even Jesus had the twelve disciples. None of them were perfect, but they each served a significant part in Jesus' life. This group of men was by His side to teach, preach, heal, and cast out demons while traveling with Him.

"Two are better than one, because they have a good return for their labor. If either of them falls down, one can help the other up. But pity anyone who falls and has no one to help them up. Also, if two lie down together, they will keep warm. But how can one keep warm alone? Though one may be overpowered,

two can defend themselves. A cord of three strands is not quick-ly broken."- Ecclesiastes 4:9-12.

Having a support system is essential to get through this journey and to fulfill God's purpose for your life. You don't need a group of people who bring you down, talk negatively, never support you, or always have drama in their lives. When you seek God, He will bring the right people into your life. They will be your bridge/help during your life journey. You need people who will push you closer to God, uplift you, encourage you, love you unconditionally and who are patient.

How Are You Living?

When my oldest son started running track in high school, I noticed he changed many of his daily habits. He said the goal was to get a college scholarship, so he started working toward it by eating healthy, exercising more, ensuring he never missed a practice, and even studying videos of various athletes in track. I noticed he has so much love for the sport he made lifestyle changes.

I wonder if we are like this when we choose to give our lives to Christ. Can people tell through our lifestyles and daily habits we represent God? It's more than just praying, wearing necklaces with a cross, wearing your best outfits on Sundays, and saying you follow Jesus. People in the world should be able to tell we are in Christ just by how we live.

There is a problem when people in the world cannot tell we are different. We are supposed to be set apart from this world, and that's why the way we act is significant. It's easy to say you believe in Jesus, but I have seen church members who won't even speak to others in the morning and have bad attitudes. People go to the clubs every Saturday night and sit in church on Sundays half asleep. Arguments break out on the street due to road rage and Christ followers curse people out all week, lie, and then are the nicest people on Sundays.

"Do not conform to the pattern of this world but be transformed by the renewing of your mind. Then you will be able to test and approve what God's will is — His good, pleasing and perfect will." - Romans 12:2

Are we human? Yes! We sin every day, so falling or making a mistake will happen throughout our lives. Yet as you get serious with your walk with Christ, doing things not of God should slowly decrease. Things like having sex before marriage, drugs, drinking, partying every weekend, cursing somebody out, or lashing out because of your anger, should no longer be your desire. Your focus will shift, and it will be all about honoring God. As you build a relationship with Jesus, He will start to work those negative things out of you.

"I, therefore, the prisoner in the Lord, beseech you to walk worthily of the calling wherewith ye were called." - Ephesians 4:1

Every day God wakes you up is a new day! So even if you have worldly habits, it's okay no need to feel judged or embarrassed. This walk with Christ is a journey, which means our Father will be working on us until the day we die. No one on this earth is perfect, and we all have issues God wants to work out for us. Yet, your goal every day should be to represent Jesus the best way you can. And if you fall, repent, and ask for the Holy Spirit's help to try again.

How Are You Waiting in This Season?

Nothing can be more agonizing than waiting for God to answer a prayer. You can be praying for an elevation in your career, a husband/wife, a new job, an increase in finances, healing of an illness, or recovery of a broken relationship; whatever the case is, waiting can feel like forever.

During the season of waiting, we should examine our attitudes and our way of thinking. How are you waiting? Do you get up every morning and praise God for what He has done and for the things you know He is going to do? Or do you get grumpy, complain non-stop and talk about how others are getting blessings except you?

One year, my friend Jonathan who worked at a firm office in Texas, was looked over for a supervisor position at his job. He was devastated and hurt, but he kept doing his best at the workplace. Jonathan never spoke negatively about the person chosen over him for the position and kept going home praying and serving God. A year later, his boss (the same guy who did not give him the supervisor position) told him he was moving to the headquarters office in New York and wanted Jonathan to take over the office and become a firm partner. So, he received a higher position and pay, but he is now in charge of the young man chosen over him for the supervisor position.

With the season of waiting, God knows what He is doing. We can be very impatient and when a waiting season comes, sometimes we forget God has better plans than us.

"For I know the plans I have for you," declares the LORD, "plans to prosper you and not harm you, plans to give you hope and a future." Jeremiah 29:11

We also need to have a cheerful heart (easier said than done), but we must keep our faith, speak positive things, and trust God.

"A cheerful heart is good medicine, but a crushed spirit dries up the bones." Proverbs 17:22

No matter what your circumstances are, continue serving God. Your posture during the waiting season matters! Don't change your attitude if the blessing you are waiting for is not coming when you expected. Don't start to think or speak negatively. Believe Jesus is who He says He is and will never fail you. God can see how you act during the waiting season, and if you have a good heart and attitude, His blessings will pour into your life.

I Don't Know About This

(It's Kind of Boring)

One day I was looking through YouTube for a church service to watch. I try my best to hear the word daily because it helps me stay on track. I came upon this video of a pastor just having a question-and-answer session with church members. This small group of people could open up and ask the pastor any questions they had about life and the Bible. During this session, a young man said to the pastor he was having a hard time being a Christ-follower because compared to all his friends who were non-believers or doing their own thing, their lifestyle seemed fun, and he felt like trying to follow all God's rules were boring. He ended his statement with, "I don't know about this; it's kind of boring."

Being saved at a young age, that was not my first-time hearing this from a person following Christ. When we hear this from individuals, let's remember not to judge them because of their perspective. We are in a world of social media and living in this culture is very hard. Many people think having fun is about doing drugs, drinking excessively, spending

35

money on designer clothes, taking expensive trips, strip clubs, or having sex with multiple partners. From a natural point of view, yes, this looks like "the good life," especially with the way it's pushed through music and social media these days.

It looks fun and tempting, but when you start to grow a relationship with God, you will understand God has rules to protect us. Without boundaries, we will fall into the traps of culture and their definition of fun.

"Do not love the world or the things in the world. If anyone loves the world, the love of the Father is not in him. For all that is in the world-the desires of the flesh and the desires of the eyes and pride in possessions is not from the Father but is from the world. And the world is passing away along with its desires, but whoever does the will of God abides forever." 1 John 2:15-17.

Jesus wants you to have lots of fun; He wants you to enjoy life. Yet He wants you to do it in a way that pleases Him and won't cause heartache and pain. Doing drugs can lead to your death or other mental problems. Being in the strip club can lead to lust. Having sex outside of marriage with multiple partners will open the door to soul ties or heartbreak. Living in sin will always have consequences, whether you can see it or not. People will always post or tell you about all the fun they had, but they will never post about the downfalls.

When you grow a relationship with God, worldly desires will slowly decrease. There was a time when I would post memes on my social media that had a lot of cussing. Now that I have a closer relationship with Jesus, I watch would I post because I know I always represent Him. You can do plenty of things for fun and still be of Christ. Traveling, movies, bowling, or group retreats don't have to involve worldly sin to make it fun. When you get into a community with other followers, you won't care about worldly things because you know there are so many ways to have fun without feeling like it's boring.

I Hate it Here BUT..........

Since I was a little girl, I have been saved and heavily in church. Throughout this journey with Jesus, I have had these "I hate it here" moments. As we go through life, we will encounter moments where we feel like life sucks. The list can go on and on from divorce, bankruptcy, childhood trauma such as abuse, molestation, loss of a loved one, being lied to, or even career issues. As followers of Christ, we go through challenging life situations, making us question why we are even here on this earth.

When I had these moments, I felt terrible because I felt God would be mad or disappointed in me for feeling like this. I know the phrases, "Things could be worse," "Be thankful for what you have," and "God wouldn't put more on you than you can bear." I heard those phrases over a thousand times, but it still did not change how I felt about being heartbroken, abandoned, or rejected. Yet I realized God knows our hearts. He knows about your feelings, and what you think, so it's okay to express to Him your genuine emotions.

Say, God, this sucks! I hate it here, and I am going through it, but You are a healer. I know You will work out any situation I am going through.

I heard this pastor say God cannot help you where you pretend to be. He can only help you where you are. Wherever you are, God is right there in the mist. He wants us to have a relationship with Him so the Holy Spirit can come in and hold us up when we are weak.

Don't be like me and feel like you have to be ashamed for feeling what you do. Jesus loves us no matter what. He wants openness from you and nothing less. Being honest allows vulnerability which will open up the door to a better connection with Jesus.

But He said to me, "My grace is sufficient for you, for My power is made perfect in weakness," Therefore I will boast all the more gladly of my weaknesses, so that the power of Christ may rest upon me. – 2 Corinthians 12:9

When you go to God, tell Him how you feel and always put a "but" in it. Sometimes we don't realize how powerful the word is when talking to Him. You saying God, I feel horrible, yet adding "BUT" is telling Him you trust Him no matter the situation.

Let's practice:

God, I am single, BUT I trust You will send me a mate when the time is right.

God, I feel rejected for not getting the job offer, BUT I trust You will open the doors to other opportunities.

God, I feel overwhelmed being in debt, BUT I know You will give me the resources to get out.

God, I feel I am not where I want to be in life right now, BUT I trust You will allow me to get where I need to be in life.

God, I feel depressed and suicidal, BUT I give You my thoughts and ask the Holy Spirit to help me through this.

See how BUT changes the narrative! Yes, you are going through a challenging trial in your life right now, yet you are saying BUT, letting Jesus know you trust Him.

Let God be Your
Roadside Service

I recall when I went shopping with my children at Target one Sunday afternoon. It was one of those scorching hot days, about 90 degrees. After we got into the car, I put my key in the ignition, only for the vehicle not to start. I kept trying and trying but nothing happened. I became overwhelmed and frustrated because it was boiling hot outside, and the children also started to complain. After telling them to go inside the building where they could get out the heat until I could get help, I stood outside sweating, trying to figure out the problem and contact the towing company. Many individuals passed me but didn't even notice I needed help, and others witnessed it, but nobody offered to assist. After about an hour, a tow guy showed up and gave me a simple jump to start my car so I could get home. As we stood outside talking, I told him everything that happened. He said something to me that stood out.

"Next time, don't try to figure it out; call us right away. We are here to help and save you from unnecessary stress."

That's how we need to think of God (Our Lord and Savior). He is our roadside assistance when drowning in life. In this lifetime, we will go through seasons of grief, confusion, disappointment, pain, loss, every type of adverse feeling we could encounter. Yet this is when we need to call on Jesus as soon as something happens.

"Do not be anxious about anything, but in every situation, by prayer and petition, with thanksgiving, present your requests to God. And the peace of God, which transcends all understanding, will guard your hearts and your minds in Christ Jesus." – Philippians 4:6-7

When life situations arrive, we try to figure it out, talk to friends/family, and plan ways to get out or through the problem. When we try to fix things on our own, this leads to us being frustrated, overwhelmed, mentally tired, or even defeated from the start; yet, in reality, all we need to do is go to God immediately.

The start of divorce, bankruptcy, loss of a family member, loss of a job, broken relationship, whatever you're going through, your first step is to call on Jesus for assistance. Please don't hold on to it; completely hand it over to Him and ask for guidance. Do not ask for the easy way out, for God to remove it, but ask Him to guide you through the situation. We sometimes encounter problems and want God to take them away immediately, but how can we grow in our relationship with God if we never go through storms?

"You are my hiding place; You will protect me from trouble and surround me with songs of deliverance. I will instruct you and teach you in the way you should go; I will counsel you with my loving eye on you." – Psalm 32:7-8

We will all break down or run into some trouble at some point in our lives, but when you make God your roadside assistance, you let Him come into your life and save you.

Make a List and Check it Twice

One day, a friend of mine was having a bad day and spent the whole day on a negative rant about everything going wrong in her life and what she wished she had. I told her the devil had a hold of her thoughts, and we needed to do something to turn her thinking around. So, I told her to make a list with two columns. On one side, she had to write down all the things she felt were not going right in her life, and on the other side, she put down all the blessings she had, including things such as having a job, money, food in the house, and a place to sleep, etcetera. After making a list, she noticed she had more things to be grateful for than she recognized at the moment.

We as humans will encounter days in which we are unsatisfied with our life situations and want things to be different. Yet, this is when you have to make a (physical or mental) list to remind yourself of God's love and the beautiful things He has already done for you. No matter how bad your situation is, you can always find a reason to praise God.

"When the peace of Christ rules in our hearts, thankfulness overflows. Even in the darkest of times, we can praise God for His love, His sovereignty, and His promise to be near us when we call."- Psalm 145:18

You will have down moments, which is okay, but the problem is you keep complaining for hours or even days. Doing this shows God you don't trust His plans or timing. He knows the desires of your heart, and you have to believe He will come through for you.

"May He grant you your heart's desire and fulfill all your plans."- Psalm 20:4

All you have to do is have faith the size of a mustard seed, and Jesus will help you through those moments when negative thoughts creep into your mind. He may not give you precisely what you ask for, but He will always provide you with what you need and exceed your expectations.

Allowing negative thoughts to control your mood or day is another enemy trick. So next time you are having a bad day or start to think about what you don't have, make a list, and check it twice. It will turn your negative thinking about your situation into praise.

Overcoming Church Hurt

Growing up in church organizations, I saw many members being judgmental and even hypocritical. I grew up watching people twist Bible verses out of context for their purposes. I also witnessed individuals say, "God told me you did this, or God told me to tell you," which I knew He did not tell them. As I became older, I stayed away from church because I saw people misuse God's words or claim to be Christ-followers on Sunday but act completely different during the weekdays.

Now I realize I suffered from church hurt. That's when people are in the church and do things not of God, and it makes you back away from the religion or quit as a whole. Many of us have been through this, seeing pastors cheat on their wives, take money from the congregations and not use it for church purposes but for self-gain. Another reason could be how judgmental and mean a lot of Christians are to others, or you feel like the church is overlooking your talents. A person can experience church hurt for various reasons.

Church hurt is attached to rejection, fear, vulnerability, hurt, loss, embarrassment, etcetera. This happens more than we think or hear about. Yet we should not let it stop us from having a relationship with God. People are human, and that's why God says to follow Him and His word because people are flawed and will make mistakes.

Don't let anything affect your relationship with God. He sees the pain and the situation that happened to you. He is with you through it all.

"Never will I leave you; never will I forsake you."- Hebrews 13:5

Go to Him and allow Him to heal the hurt you encountered at that place of worship. If it's one person, ask Him to help you forgive and see if you can continue to move past the issue. If it's multiple people, ask God to reveal if this church is the right location for you. See the thing about our Father is if you ask Him, He will provide.

"Until now, you have not asked for anything in My name. Ask and you will receive, and your joy will be complete."- John 16:24

This verse tells you God listens and is ready to answer; all you have to do is ask. Understand you need a place of worship and community, to connect with other followers so you can build relationships with them and come together to do God's work on this earth. We are not meant to be here alone; God wants us to break bread and share our burdens.

So, take all your church hurt and give it to God; He will heal you and tell you what you need to do next. Don't stop going to church or allow negative thoughts about the church to cloud your mind. Despite what you may feel, every church is not the same, and one person nor group of people represents a whole church nor Christ.

Prayer is Prayer

My children and I pray together every morning. When they were younger, one morning, my youngest son, who was five years old, complained we did not pray the usual lengthy prayer. He said it because our prayer was short, he was worried God wouldn't hear it. I had to take the opportunity to let him know prayer is prayer.

God does not care how long or short your prayers are; He wants them to come from the heart and be genuine. I have grown up in church atmospheres and have seen many people pray. I witnessed an hour-long prayer that did not move the crowd, and I have seen ten-minute prayers that would have the congregation on their knees. Powerful prayers come from the heart and not just words.

"When you pray, you are not to be like the hypocrites: for they love to stand and pray in the synagogues and on the street corners so that they may be seen by men. Truly I say to you, they have their reward in full. But when you pray, go into your room, close the door, and pray to your Father, who is unseen. Then your Father, who sees what is done in secret, will reward you. And when you pray, do not keep on babbling like pagans,

for they think they will be heard because of their many words.
Do not be like them, for your Father knows what you need be-
fore you ask Him."- Matthew 6:5-8

There should be no judgment on quick or long prayers. There are times you will need to spend hours in prayer and moments where you have to say a quick one throughout the day. Our heavenly Father is looking at your heart when you come to Him. Are you saying a prayer to check off your daily list of things to do? Or are you seeking God with an open heart?

So, whether you pray today for five minutes, twenty minutes, or hours, length doesn't matter, but the quality of the prayer does. If you don't know how to pray, ask God to guide you and read the Bible so He can teach you. He knows what you want and need, so be honest and don't think about the length of time when praying, but its meaning.

Sitting in a Mess, While Others are Getting Blessed

Have you ever encountered certain seasons where it appears everyone around you is getting blessed but you? You scroll down your social media timeline, and everyone is receiving new job positions, cars, an increase in finances, or getting engaged. Meanwhile, your heart desires to get married, but you can't even get a text back, or it seems like the dating pool is so shallow you will never find your "soul mate." You have prayed, fasted, read your Bible daily, but it seems like those (you feel) who barely talk to God get the things your heart desire?

This season can suck, and it can make you feel sad or defeated, but you must understand God is working in your favor even when you don't see it.

"For I know the plans I have for you," declares the LORD, "plans to prosper you and not to harm you, plans to give you hope and a future. – Jeremiah 29:11

First, let me say this: you are not alone when you have these emotions. Many people are currently experiencing the same feelings during these seasons. The problem occurs when you stay in this emotion. Yes, we are all human, but we must learn to steer our emotions in the right direction.

When you observe someone receive a blessing you have been praying for, stop and thank God.

For example, you are a married woman who has suffered several miscarriages, but you witness another woman being able to conceive and experience a full-term pregnancy. Stop and say this:

Dear God, thank you for blessing (the person's name). Seeing this, I know You are real and if You did it for them, You will do it for me.

This simple prayer to God will help you change your emotions from sad to grateful; it will stop you from going down the dark hole of negative emotions, and it shows Jesus you trust Him.

"And without faith, it is impossible to please Him, for whoever would draw near to God must believe that He exists and that He rewards those who seek Him." Hebrews 11:6

Never get envious, jealous, or sad when others get the things you have been praying for. That's a sign your blessing is close. If you haven't been on the right path, ask for forgiveness, and seek Jesus with all your heart. Remember, when you spend time with Him, He will direct your path in perfect timing. So never get distressed when you are sitting in a mess, but others are getting blessed. That's a sign your blessing is right around the corner. Continue to have faith and stay encouraged.

Spreading God's Love

Years ago, I was in line at Starbucks getting a coffee. At the time, I was going through a healing process from a difficult breakup, so I was having a rough day. After ordering, I was behind this lady who seemed to be at the first window, where you wait a little longer than average. I started to get a little irritated when I noticed her showing the cashier at the window her phone (in which she was showing him a coupon). So, in my mind, I am just thinking she is holding up the line to get a discount on her purchase. As I approached the window, I pulled out my debit card to pay, and the cashier told me the lady in front of me had paid for my order. The feeling I had inside me brought so much joy due to her actions. At that moment, my heartbreak did not matter, and I felt the love of God. I wanted to pass around that feeling to others from that day on.

God placed her in my path. Her simple gesture changed the course of my day and made me look at the sky and say, "God, I know that was you." How often do you try and show others God's goodness when you go out?

The earth is hurting, and people are going through so much pain. Making small gestures like paying for someone's meal or gas, opening doors, helping someone put groceries on their card, giving a single mother a gift card, or even complimenting someone can change their day and show God's love.

"So then, as we have opportunity, let us do good to everyone, and especially to those who are of the household of faith." - Galatians 6:10

Being nice to others will always show people a glimpse of Jesus' love He has for all of us. You don't have to give someone money to be friendly; a simple compliment or small gesture can change a person's life. As followers of Christ, we were placed on this earth to spread the gospel, love, and fulfill his purpose. Spreading the gospel can also cover showing others kindness. So, every day you wake up, ask God to show you ways you can spread His love. Whether big or small, kind gestures can place a smile on someone's face and make them see the goodness of our heavenly Father.

Surviving the Pain for a Reason

I have witnessed a lady forced with the choice of having to remove her ten-year-old son from life support due to brain damage from a car accident involving a drunk driver. This tragic event would break anyone's heart or even shake up their faith. We came across each other's paths about a year later and I found out she started an organization supporting parents who have lost a child due to drunk drivers. She took all her pain and turned it into a blessing for others. When I spoke to her, she said through the grace of God, she was able to cope with the pain and she would take all her heartbreak and help others get through their tragic storms.

We will never fully understand why people encounter unfortunate experiences during their lifetime. Situations include losing a parent, being diagnosed with cancer, getting laid off from a job, having a loved one walk out on a marriage, and having someone you trusted lie and betray you. The list of painful situations in life can go on. Yet, we need to take all our pains and hand them over to God for us to heal.

"Why? Because we rely on Him. We know that He gives us far more then we can handle, but when yoked with Him, He can handle the burden." -Matthew 11:28-30

You will encounter situations that will knock you down and rob you of joy in this lifetime. Some trials will be more challenging than others and will even weaken your faith. Yet 's when Jesus draws closer to you. He has chosen you because he knows you are a warrior and His child. He also wants you to take the experience and the pain to help others get through it.

"In all this, you greatly rejoice, though now for a little while you may have had to suffer grief in all kinds of trials." - 1 Peter 1:6

We often think our storms are all about us, and maybe we went through them to help others. Your testimony about your heartbreak or situation can help someone through the process or even stop them from taking their own lives. I have seen how people sharing their testimonies stopped a person from committing suicide because someone else shared their experience and how they got through the pain.

You survived it for a reason; share with others about the divorce, childhood trauma, bankruptcy, loss of a child, and other issues so you can help someone with their pain.

The Art of Letting Go

H ave you ever noticed the meme on social media where Jesus is kneeling in front of the little girl while holding a big bear behind his back? He asks the girl to give him the small bear she holds, but she won't give it up because she says she loves it. Everyone looking at the meme can see God has something more significant for her, but she can't see it.

This example is how many of us act toward God regarding dating. We are involved with someone He is asking us to release from our lives, but being hard-headed, we choose not to. There are various reasons we won't let go: fear of nothing better coming, insecurities, self-esteem (afraid you can't do better), being comfortable, etcetera.

This is when you have to learn to trust God because He shows you these "red flags" for a reason. I hear many people say phrases like, "Something is not right," "I have a gut feeling," or "my intuition is telling me." That's all the Holy Spirit. He is guiding you, showing you these things so you can learn and leave the person alone before encountering unnecessary problems and heartaches.

"For I know the plans I have for you," declares the Lord, "plans to prosper you and not harm you, plans to give you a

hope and future." - Jeremiah 29:11

God has a plan for you, and who you date or marry will either allow you to fulfill His purpose or delay/destroy it. Growing a relationship with Jesus, especially when dating, is very important. If they pull you away from Christ, always speak negatively, don't contribute to your happiness, have drama, or don't have goals or vision, it's time to seek God for clarification. Ask Him to reveal if this person is right for you during this season, and if He has already given you signs to let go and you can't, then ask Him for assistance with that. God can do anything; all you have to do is request, and He will give you the strength to let go and trust He has something more extraordinary.

The Body is Good but What About the Soul?

We exist in a society driving for the perfect body image. Social media pushes everyone to have flawless skin, no wrinkles, a flat stomach, a slim body with no percentage of any fat anywhere, and women shaped like Coca-Cola bottles.

Social media platforms and magazines push this agenda and can be seen everywhere you go. Many people spend thousands of dollars on cosmetic surgery to achieve their body goals. Yet they often solely focus on the physical aspect, neglecting the spiritual side.

Individuals spend time daily exercising (gym or outdoors), paying for weight loss/enhancing products, or making sure they eat healthily but neglect to open a Bible, pray, or spend time with God. Looking suitable outside is important, but God cares more about your soul and heart than anything else.

I have seen and met people who look gorgeous on the outside but are unattractive on the inside. They are mean, gossip, lie, cheat, steal, put others down and act very cold-hearted.

"A man who is kind benefits himself, but a cruel man hurts himself." – Proverbs 11:17

Do you suppose God would be delighted with somebody who had a fabulous body but was always mean to others or someone who had an average body but a loving heart? Christ-followers should invest in praying, reading the word, worshipping, and spending time with our heavenly Father. It doesn't even have to be complicated; you can take five minutes out of your day and set aside for God. We must remember there is life after this, so what we do and how we act matters.

"What good will it be for someone to gain the whole world yet forfeit their soul? Or what can anyone give in exchange for their soul?" – Matthew 16:26

What good is it for you to have thousands of social media followers, have a great body, and have a broken soul? There's nothing wrong with investing in your body but don't forget to invest in your soul.

Unplug From Social Media and Plug Into God

I remember a period when I had a friend complaining non-stop about not being happy in her life. She did not have the career she wanted, was single, and felt lonely. To make things worse, she would scroll on social media every day and complain about how everyone else had a relationship but her.

The situation she was going through is widespread. How often do we scroll on social media feeling sad or some type of way when we see someone else has the things we desire? It could be a person getting a job, a raise, a new car, a house, traveling on expensive vacations, or even announcing their engagement. It's a part of our human nature to get envious of others. Yet we must remember what God has for us will always be for us.

"Do not covet your neighbor's wife, his male or female slave, his ox or donkey, or anything that belongs to your neighbor." – Exodus 20:17

We will have moments when we look at what someone else has accomplished and think, "I wish I had..." The problem comes when viewing another person's blessing negatively affects your emotions. When you see couples or families on vacation, individuals post their accomplishments, and you get sad, jealous, or angry, that's the time you need to unplug.

When you are not happy with the way things are going in your life, social media only adds fuel to the fire. Scrolling for hours can be damaging if you are in a hurt season. Taking breaks or limiting your time on social media can help you get through this season of unhappiness.

Unplug from social media and get closer to God. Social media can be a negative gateway to sadness, envy, and depression. Therefore, until you get into a good space where you can be on a social site and it doesn't affect your emotions, unplug.

Take the energy of scrolling and plug into God. He can heal you from the emptiness you feel, and He is the only one who can bless you with the things your heart desires. Also, spending time with God will allow you to better your relationship. He is our Lord and Savior, and He has all the answers you are looking for. Why would you want to keep getting sad when you can plug into Jesus and get healed and happy? So, take frequent breaks, unplug from social platforms, and plug into the main source, God.

Wanting Love in All the Wrong Places

I watch this show called, "For My Man," a television series about women previously or currently incarcerated due to helping their men commit crimes. I noticed all of the women who had the opportunity to speak about their cases stated the same thing. They claimed to have gotten involved because they did not love themselves, had low self-esteem, and just wanted love from someone.

You might judge and think you would never go this far to be loved, but many of us do in a different way. Engaging in situations such as sleeping with someone else's spouse, dating someone we know is not suitable for us because we don't want to be alone, allowing people to run over us, or even being a people pleaser (always saying yes) is the same thing. You don't have to be on the level of doing crime but compromising yourself for love and attention is just as dangerous.

"Come to Me all you who are weary and burdened, and I will give you rest." - Matthew 11:28

We all have had a season of heartbreak or disappointment. Many circumstances that occur in life can mess up your self-esteem. Situations such as divorce, breakups, childhood trauma, abuse, and being neglected can all influence your choices. Unhealed pain can lead to poor decisions, causing more problems and heartache.

"If any of you lacks wisdom, you should ask God, who gives generously to all without finding fault, and it will be given to you."- James 1:5

Wanting to be loved is not bad; God said it's not good to be alone. Yet He wants us to be loved and get attention the right way. We can only do this if we seek God first and learn His ways. His love is more powerful than any love or attention you can get from someone. So, if you have broken parts of you, give it to Him and ask Him to help you make better choices with it comes to wanting love, validation, or attention.

Watch Your Mouth; God Can Hear You

I knew this lady who was a close friend of my mother, and one day, we were outside just having a conversation. She asked me about my love life, and I told her I had given up and would be single for the rest of my life. She suddenly interrupted me with a strong voice and said, "Watch your mouth; God can hear you!"

At first, in my mind, I believed she was being overly dramatic because it wasn't that serious, but when she explained why she stated that, I understood.

My mother's friend talked about the power of the tongue and how a person needs to watch what they say because that's what they are manifesting. She also said you unintentionally tell God you don't trust Him or His word when you speak negatively aloud.

"Death and life are in the power of the language, and they that love it shall eat the fruit thereof." -Proverbs 18:21

I never looked at my actions in that way. I was so accustomed to speaking negatively about that portion of my life that I just gave up hope.

We are all human and have our moments, but that's when we need to turn to God. Tell Him you are struggling and losing hope in a specific area in your life, and you need Him to restore your faith.

Maybe you have been applying to jobs left and right with no answer, been praying for a marriage that seems to keep getting worse, feel like you will never get out of debt, or you could have been praying to have a child but still haven't conceived.

Whatever the case is, make sure that you say positive things anytime you speak on that subject.

When you speak on your situation, just keep saying that God will work it out, even if you doubt it at the moment.

"If you can?" said, Jesus. "Everything is possible for one who believes." Mark 9:23

Remember, all Jesus is asking you for is a tiny mustard seed of trust.

"Because you have so little faith. Truly I tell you, if you have faith as small as a mustard seed, you can stay to the mountain, 'Move from here to there,' and it will move. Nothing will be impossible for you." Matthew 17:20

He knows what you are facing, and He knows what you feel. You just must give it to Him and trust Him fully. So, keep believing and remember to watch your mouth.

What Are You Looking At?

I was sitting at a restaurant having dinner with my friend, and during our time together, I discussed my feelings on my upcoming birthday. In my mind, when I hit the age of thirty-five, I thought I would have everything together. I would be living in a big house, working in my dream career, married, and have a good income, where I can afford to take many vacations each year. Yet, instead, I felt I had failed in life since I had not accomplished those goals. During my "complaining sessions" of how unhappy I was, my friend interrupted me, and said, "What are you looking at?" He then tells me how far I have come in life, the degrees I have, all the good things I have done in my life, and the people I have helped while being a single mom.

How many of us are like this? We look at all the things we need to do or do not have instead of realizing where we are and how far God has brought us. We look at all the negative things, such as not being in a relationship, not having the finances we want or the house we desire, even the dream career.

When these moments come, we need to stop and change our focus. No, you are not in your dream house, but you have a roof over your head. You are not married, but this is the time to get closer to God and enjoy your singleness. Your business is not as successful as you thought it would be, but you took the first step and became an entrepreneur. You may not have your dream job, but you are employed at the moment, and in God's timing, if it is His will, He will open the door to the desires of your heart.

I know it's hard, especially when your life is not going how you envisioned it, or you see everyone around you getting the blessings you have been praying for.

"Give thanks in all circumstances; for this is the will of God in Christ Jesus for you." -1 Thessalonians 5:18

I don't care how bad things get in your life. Do your best to find at least one thing a day to be thankful for. Being grateful and having faith in God pleases Him.

"And without faith it is impossible to please God, because anyone who comes to Him must believe that He exists and He rewards those who earnestly seek Him." – Hebrew 11:6

You are human; God knows you will have obstacles in your life that will have you feeling defeated or sad. He knows your needs, your wants, and desires. He needs you to have faith in Him. He will provide for you in due time and you will be thankful in the process.

Every day, God wakes you up. Before you start to complain, find at least one thing to be thankful for and change what you are looking at.

Who Are You? Identity Crisis

I came across this video on YouTube where a young lady talked about her years in college. She was a popular cheerleader, had an athlete boyfriend, was a part of a sorority, and was known for having high spirits on campus. Unfortunately, she got into a bad car accident her senior year. Her injuries were so bad she lost her right leg and an eye. Once returning to school, people barely talked to her; the same friends she had didn't come around anymore. Also, she would get strange looks on campus, and her boyfriend left her. After graduating, she realized people were only attaching themselves to her because of her popularity. She also stated she felt like a nobody since she was no longer a cheerleader when this happened.

Many people are like this because they allow what they do to define who they are. Yet we have to understand the things we do are just job titles from a spouse, athlete, lawyer, doctor, therapist, police officer, etcetera. We do those things, but it's not who we are. We are God's children and followers of Christ.

God created us in His image so we could share His overflowing love, grace, and goodness here on earth. It's essential to know and understand the difference, titles are what we do, but Christ-followers are who we are. So even if there is a shift change in your title, you won't fall into a depression or an identity crisis because you know whom you belong to.

"And He gave the apostles, the prophets, the evangelists, the shepherds, and teachers, to equip the saints for the work of ministry, for building up the body of Christ." – Ephesians 4:11-12

Titles on earth are vital; it's a part of you and your passion. Yet we have to remember it's what we do, not who we are. Who we are is followers of Christ, and our main goal is to serve Him and fulfill the plans He has for us? So, when someone asks what you do, let them know and then tell them who you are.

Wrong Address, I do Not Live There Anymore

I spoke to a friend the other day who poured out her frustration because she turned her life over to Christ, yet she had issues from her past that kept appearing. Every time she spoke the gospel around some of her family or friends, they would shut her down and bring up past offenses like her addiction to smoking and selling marijuana (weed). She said, "I wish they would stop because I don't live there anymore."

How many of us have the same issue? We have given our lives to God while trying to do right, but people around us continue bringing up what we use to do or who we used to be.

Therefore, if anyone is in Christ, he is a new creation. The old has passed away, behold, the new has come. - 2 Corinthians 5:17

When feeling frustrated, you must remember God's words. Just because individuals from your past don't see the new creation you have become doesn't mean anything; it's all about what God sees.

When the past keeps being brought up, it can lead to discouragement, having a person feeling helpless or trapped. This can also significantly affect those who are just starting off their walk in Christ.

With situations like this, you initially need to check your circle. When someone you barely see says something about what you use to do, it does not affect you as much as it would if it is a close friend or family member. When you give your life to Christ, you may have to change up your circle or who you associate with. This is when you seek God and ask Him to place individuals in your life to support your journey and remove those who won't.

This includes family members as well. Do not get it twisted; family can discourage you from the process of walking in Christ when they keep bringing up who you used to be. Recognize it's okay to distance yourself from them as well. I am not saying cut them off completely; I am saying do not be around them as often as you use to.

A little side note: Do not cut off people unless you seek permission or wisdom from God. We sometimes get mad at individuals who say stuff, and we want to automatically cut them off. Yet sometimes God wants to show those around you His power through your life and actions. If people saw how someone's life was transformed through Christ, it can make them desire their own personal relationship with God.

Never let people who keep bringing up your past discourage you. You just need to continue spreading God's word, keep spreading love, keep doing good, and testifying. People will say what you use to do or how you use to act. When they bring up old negative memories, cross it out, and reject it in your mind (return to sender) because you do not live there anymore.

Final Thoughts

Throughout this journey called life, everyone will face hardships and situations that will test their faith. You will have seasons where you fully trust God and experience other seasons where you feel like he has completely left you. Understand that he will never leave your side and has already defeated any storms you will face; you have to trust and believe in him. This 30-day devotional is for those who need some encouragement during life's hardships. Take that heartbreak, divorce, miscarriage, anxiety, broken heart, insecurities, bankruptcy, lack of support, childhood trauma, or whatever has hurt you, and give God all your broken pieces. All those circumstances have left you with damaged parts of your life. He will take that brokenness to restore, bless you, and strengthen your relationship with him.

"The Lord is near to the brokenhearted and saves the crushed in spirit" - Psalm 34:18.

Remember God keeps his promises, and he says if you take the first step in trusting him, he will carry you the rest of the way.

About the Author

Jelia Coleman- Hepner is a native of Fayetteville, NC. This mother of three has been writing poetry in her journals since she was twelve. She obtained her bachelor's in mass communications and master's in journalism to sharpen her skills and craft in writing. After graduation, she started her radio career and worked for a local newspaper. She developed her passion for writing news coverage, blogs, and reviews during this time. As a writer, she has covered many events from news to politics and won the ACHI magazine 2018 award for journalist of the year. Jelia also intends to use her passion and talents to encourage others during this life journey. Inspiring others, spending time with her children, and traveling, are the things she enjoys.